ON THE PLATFORM

A student talks to God

DAVID GATWARD

Kevin
Mayhew

First published in 1996 by
KEVIN MAYHEW LTD
Rattlesden
Bury St Edmunds
Suffolk IP30 0SZ

© 1996 David J. Gatward and
Kevin Mayhew Limited

ISBN 086209 758 4
Catalogue No 1500040

Typesetting & Page Creation by BluePrint Group (UK) Ltd.
Cover Illustration by Lorraine White

CONTENTS

For Roz . . . .
"Together times are fun times"
(Winnie the Pooh)

ACKNOWLEDGEMENTS

Mum and Dad: For being my Mum and Dad.

John: For being so confident in my work that you believe the reading of my books to be unnecessary! (That is except for this page to see if your name has been mentioned!)

James: For teaching me how to use this flippin' computer!

Marti: Cheers for checking the prayers and making sure I never ended up sounding too much like a Pink Floyd song! ('Hurrah!' for 'The Sewers of Society' and 'Cellophane Sunshine'!)

Trev (alias John Travolta!): Who knows? Now that you are mentioned in this book you'll become famous and thus be able to afford your own clothes instead of using mine all the time!

Jim: For all that essential male bonding down at the gym! 'RAAH!'

Ian: How do you manage to be so continuously funny all the time?!

Clive: For being a great room mate, supplying me with scooby snacks and all the quotes from 'Star Wars' and putting up with my scungyness! 'Nite Clive!'

Marcus: To make up for the spelling mistake in the last one! You LAAAARD!

All my friends at college: Cheers for some great years!

Charlotte Mason College: Not only will you (hopefully!) provide me with a degree but also plenty of memories which will always make me laugh!

David Kossoff: If I hadn't read your book I'd not be here now. Thanks for providing me with the inspiration.

Frank Topping: For your encouragement and advice.

Anthia Morton-Senna: For taking me seriously.

Mum's Amazing Savoury Mince: Without this truly astounding recipe, the 'Brow Boys' would have faded away!

Deep Purple: The music behind my madness!

INTRODUCTION

My time at college up to now has been rather interesting to say the least. To date I have managed to live on very poor food indeed, drink lots and lots of beer, have far too many hangovers, break a wardrobe, melt my room-mate's stereo system, annoy thousands with loud music, be reported to the college principal for having the untidiest room (on more than one occasion!), develop glandular fever, decide to leave college about four thousand times, wear very sad clothes, join a 'really good' band, be reported to the police whilst practising with said band, grow amazing sideboards and a rather cool goatee, have extremely long hair, get thrown out of my house for 'walking up the stairs too loudly' (!?!), spend all my money, avoid going to lectures, produce wonderful three thousand word essays the night before they were due in, be banned from playing my drum kit because it could be heard in the hotel down the road — and much, much more! Just your normal run-of-the-mill college student!

So why the book? And judging by the photo on the back, why buy it when the author looks like that?! Well, as a few of you will know, this is now my third book. I began writing prayers when I had just finished my first year at sixth form. I had not found it easy, and as explained in my first book, *Can we talk, Lord?*, I discovered that writing my prayers down was a way of putting down my thoughts in front of God and looking for an answer. The prayers in this book display very clearly the things going through my mind at the time and to be honest I sometimes find it quite painful to read as I see in print all of the emotions and worries I was feeling then.

The second book was written later on after I'd spent a year working as an instructor at an outdoor centre before leaving to go to college. The prayers and thoughts in this one (*A Bunch of Green Bananas!*) were more grown up, but I felt that at times the book was trying too hard to provide answers and be a little bit clever! I think that it was because I was still in utter disbelief that I had already had one published and that I was now doing my second! It went to my head a little, resulting in me trying a bit too hard. Instead of writing what I felt, I wrote what I thought needed to be written. (That's not to say that I don't think it's any good!)

This one has finally come about after a bit of a break from the old quill! College takes up a lot of your time and writing gets pushed to one side. This did however allow me to reassess what I wanted from my next book and also gave me plenty of opportunity to experience things which would provide me with some great writing material! So, after much pushing and shoving from friends and family, the pen was refilled, the computer switched on and I started to scrawl down my thoughts.

So here it is. A book of my thoughts from the things I have been through and am still experiencing at college. A collection of prayers which are real; not written solely for this book. What I have written are my feelings good and bad, worries, anxieties and those issues which I have had to tackle at college. I'm not saying that within its pages lie all the answers to your troubles. Far from it! What I hope you will find is that all these things, no matter how large or small, can be prayed about. Some of the words may not be correct. The views may not be what we should think. But they are real.

We all experience life in a variety of colours. We get told what we should do and what we should think from so many different corners — our homes, our friends, our colleges, our churches. But in the silence of our minds we tackle the permitted and the forbidden. We scream and shout for the answers. We turn the wrong way and do the wrong things. We spend our lives travelling down the wrong roads and get ignored or condemned if we argue a different point of view or go a different way. But it is only through these experiences, these thoughts, that we can discover for ourselves the right way. It is by going against the flow that so many of us do, in time, find the real answers and the outstretched hand of God.

ON THE PLATFORM

Well, Lord, this is it . . .
    the big step.
I'm off to Uni.
Doesn't seem to be real to be honest,
    standing here,
    suitcase and guitar in hand,
    tickets in my pocket,
    one way . . .
Is this happening?

I remember sitting at home,
    choosing.
Where do I go?
What do I want to do?
And Lord, I'm still pretty unsure.
Everyone else appears to know where they
    are going, and why they are going there.
Yet I seem to be more confused about
    which platform I should be on.
(This is the right one isn't it, Lord? You've
    a better view than me.)

Where am I going, Lord?
I remember the visiting day,
    the interview,
    massive buildings,
    people everywhere.

It felt like being back at primary school,
    that first day,
    clutching my bag,
    footsteps echoing down the corridor
    which towered above me,
    all the other children looking,
    staring at the new boy,
    led into a room of strangers.

And now, a few years on,
I'm back there
    in that corridor
    with my bag . . .

eighteen years down the road and
    everything I own and need in one bag;
    odd that;
    leaving so much behind —
    all the unnecessaries —
    kneeling on the floor of my room
    deciding what to leave,
    what to take:
    photos of friends,
    of family;
    tapes,
    CD's.
    (. . . and that teddy I was given when I
    was one — but don't tell anybody).

I don't feel prepared.

I should be.
I've worked for this;
 passed my exams . . . sort of . . .
 all to get here,
 to this platform,
 this little piece of tarmac that I'll soon
 step off on to a train going one way,
 away from home,
 family,
 places I know,
 places I grew up with,
 to a place which is new,
 alien,
 unexplored,
 exciting,
 frightening,
 full of questions.
Will I cope?
Will I understand?
What's the beer like?
Will I know where the toilets are?
(. . . and will I be able to find them in the
 middle of the night, in the dark with a
 hangover?)

Here's the train, Lord.
This is it.
Once my feet are on board, I'm off.
Pick up my life in a bag and on to that train.
Sit next to someone I don't know.

Watch childhood places whizz past the
    window;
    allowing myself to be taken to that big
    new place with the long dark corridors,
    strange faces and funny smells,
    as I clutch my bag and step into
    a new world.

Lord . . .

Hold my hand . . .

Amen.

MY NEW ROOM

I'm here,
    in my new room,
    in the college I chose,
    sitting on my bed,
    staring at the pink walls,
    the sounds of strangers
    filtering through under the door,
    strangers who will soon become friends
    as our, until now,
    separate lives
    connect.

Faces that I've never seen,
I'll recognise.

Voices that I've never heard,
I'll listen to.

So I just thought that I'd sit here,
    on my own,
    and settle a bit.
In my new room . . .

My new room.

It's an odd place, Lord.
It feels a bit like a prison cell crossed with

a hospital ward;
small,
cold,
full of stuff that is mine to use for the
duration:

two beds,
two desks,
two wardrobes
and a sink.

Not exactly four star,
    not exactly home.

The carpet's worn.
The paint is chipped.
The taps are leaking.

Nice curtains though;
    nice and brown.
Well, brown in the places that aren't
    see-through.

This bed is terrible:
    three springs,
    all in the middle.
(Maybe I'll take the other one, seeing as my
    room-mate isn't here yet.)

It is hard to believe,

16

that this small,
four sided,
rabbit hutch sized room
is now my home.

Home used to be where there was a
    bathroom that was warm,
    a front room with an open fire,
    a garden at the back,
    family to talk to,
    dogs to take for a walk.

Now it is this.

The bathroom is at the end of the corridor.
The floors are sticky and the showers
    already have mud in them.
A common room with a pool table,
    coke machine,
    condom machine
    and bar.
A piece of grass in the courtyard that
    hasn't been mown for at least three
    months,
    and people to talk to that I haven't even
    met yet.

Home.
My new room.

I remember getting my own room for the
    first time at home;
    my own room for my own things,
    a place for me,
    my space.

And now it's in reverse.

My new room is also
    someone else's new room:
    a someone else with fears,
    anxieties,
    apprehensions;
    a someone with stories to tell;
    a someone who will share my time,
    my life;
    a stranger who will become a friend;
    a mate.

In the new room
    which to us both
    is
    'My new room'.

And Lord,
    in this,
    my new room,
    I speak to you in the silence of my
    uncertainty
    as I sit in the anticipation of

the next part of my life;
a part I have chosen to follow,
a part I have no map for.

Guide me . . .
   in this
   my new room.

Amen.

ROOM-MATE

Lord,
  it's arrived.

My room-mate.

Someone I've never met,
  seen,
  spoken to,
  or thought about,
  here,
  in my room —
  my life.

Doesn't seem long since I had to fill in that
  form:
Do you smoke?
Do you stay up late?
Do you drink a lot?
Did you blah blah blah . . . ?

So if I answered all of those,
  why have I been put with this person?!
He has short hair!
He's dressed neatly!
A computer?
He has a computer?!
And just look at the size of that stereo!

(I'm glad I left mine at home.)
Still,
I was here first, so I get the comfiest bed!

I really can't believe that they've put us
    together.
No doubt he's thinking exactly the same.
Just look at us!
Talk about different!
How can we have anything in common,
    anything to talk about?
We have to spend a whole year in each
    other's pockets
    and we look poles apart.

(He even has a suit, Lord . . . !)

Still,
    who knows?
By tonight we'll be propping up the bar,
    getting to know each other,
    laughing,
    chatting,
    and drinking some more . . .

Well, at least I 'hope' that is what will
    happen . . .

Maybe this time next year we'll be looking
    back on our first year and remembering,

reminiscing
about all the laughs,
all the daft things we did . . .
(or I did)
. . . getting letters from the principal
about the state of our room perhaps,
setting off the fire alarm,
. . . accidentally,
eating obscene amounts of toast in the
early hours of the morning,
growing mould.

Who knows . . . ?

Help us both, Lord.
It's not easy making friends,
    especially when you have no choice,
    no option.

We've been thrust together
    into this small room;
    and we now have to share our lives.

Help us to help each other as we face this
    unknown year
    as strangers,
    and guide us
    as we begin this new journey
    into this unknown.

Amen.

FRESHERS' WEEK — THE AFTERMATH!

It's Saturday, Lord.
    . . . at least I think it is.

I'm lying on my bed in this,
    my new room.

My room-mate is on the floor,
    fully clothed and
    fast asleep!

My eyes are closed . . .
    not because I'm tired. It's just that if I
    open them the room spins, I feel sick
    and my head explodes.

The backs of my eyelids are covered in
    faint little flashing stars and my mouth
    feels like a sewer.

I also appear to be wearing my boxers on
    the outside of my jeans and my shoes
    are on the wrong feet!

And why is there a traffic cone in the
    corner of the room?

What on earth happened last night?
It's been freshers' week, Lord,
    lots of parties,
    lots of new faces,
    lots of beer.

And whisky,
    and wine,
    and more whisky,
    and . . .

Oh mate, my head . . .

It feels as if there's a herd of elephants
    inside my head doing a waltz.

What was I doing last night, Lord?
And looking at my room-mate;
    what were we both doing last night?!

Why did I drink so much, Lord?
You invented alcohol,
    but why did you give it such horrible
    after-effects?
Remember the story where you turned
    water into wine?
Good job you weren't there last night!
We sure didn't need any extra!
It was a good night, though:
    lots of music,
    lots of laughs,

everyone relaxing and getting to know
each other.
And my room-mate?
Well,
the man's entirely mad!
Did a well wicked dance on stage too!

Looks like we'll get on rather well!

But Lord,
there are so many of us here;
so many new faces.
It's all rather scary really.
Freshers' week has been great,
lots of fun,
laughs,
. . . and headaches . . .

But is all of college life like this?
How will I afford it?
What about the lectures?
Will I manage the work?

We met the tutors today.
They seem okay,
but will I be able to do what they ask of
me?

I realise I hardly know anyone yet,
but everyone still seems to be more
confident than I am;

know where they are going,
where the rooms are,
even when the essays have to be handed
in!

(Just how DO you write an essay, Lord?!)

All these thoughts are running around in
my head
panicking me.
Am I in the right place?
Have I made the right decision?
And this headache, Lord . . . !

Lord,
I hope that I'll cope;
do the work;
find the correct rooms;
join in.
I pray that I've made the right choice;
that here I'll find a purpose,
a direction.
And that when I feel lost and confused,
you'll find me and let me know that I'm
okay.

Oh,
and if I'm at the pub, Lord,
remind me never, *ever* to mix whisky
and red wine again!

Amen.

THE FOOD

In front of me, Lord, is what college
    describes as
      'My Lunch'.
On the board in lovely poetic scrawl were
    the words,
      'Spaghetti bolognaise followed by apple
      crumble and custard.'
And here it sits
    in front of me.
And I have to eat it.

I don't want to, Lord.

The spaghetti bolognaise looks like runny
    chocolate sauce on a very hard meringue
    base.
And the apple crumble should be
    re-named,
'Apple derelict and fallen down, with white
    water.'

This is dinner?
Who are they kidding?

I'm quite sure, Lord, that if I were you and
    I could see what they had done with this
    small bit of my creation, I'd be tempted

to send down one or two bolts of
   sporadic lightning!

How can they serve this?
How can they cook so badly?
I've paid for this and all I get is slop!

It amazes me how an individual can cook
   something entirely devoid of taste.
Not just bland,
   but no taste whatsoever!
Oh for a bottle of Tabasco sauce to add
   some flavour to this apple suicide!

I missed breakfast because I was up late.
And now,
   starving,
I am faced with the food equivalent of a
   bomb site.

I don't think I'll be going back for seconds.

What I'd do for my mum's cooking now;
   meat pie and potatoes,
   real apple crumble,
   stew and dumplings,
   anything but this.

Am I ungrateful, Lord?
I don't mean to be.

I know that there are people starving in the
    world;
    others living on nothing but the simplest
    of foods;
    no choice,
    eat or die.

But here I have my food made for me,
    served to me,
    and I complain.
Would I complain if I hadn't eaten for
    days?
If I had nothing to live on but rice from an
    aid station?
If I'd spent all day working in the fields to
    gather enough rice for the evening meal?

Would I complain then?

I'm sorry, Lord.
I don't want to be ungrateful.
Being brought up with food always there,
    always tasty,
    you get complacent,
    fussy.
I know that I shouldn't.
I know that I'm lucky,
    fortunate.

Help me to remember those worse off than
    myself.

That even though the apple crumble wasn't
    and the spaghetti tasted like a spare
    tyre,
    I *am* fortunate.

(But I really can't eat the carrot bits, Lord.)

Amen.

MISSING HOME

Lord,
    I've got to college,
    passed all the grades,
    settled in,
    made friends,
    handed in an essay or two,
    (honest);
    and now,
    sitting here on my own,
    I miss my home,
    my family,
    my friends.

I'm happy here, Lord.
It's just that every now and again
    I get a twinge,
    a pulling inside,
    and my mind drifts back along that road,
    the road home.

The oddest thing of all though, Lord,
    is that it isn't the big things you miss,
    but the small:

    the way that my bedroom door always
    creaked;
    that dodgy floor board that gave me
    away on so many late nights.

Why miss that?

The chill in the bathroom, early morning,
   when dad had left the window open all
   night;
   no hot water left, thanks to my brother
   spending about three days in the
   shower;

   the smell of home-made bread hitting
   your nose as you walk in to the house;
   a log fire crackling and laughing in the
   hearth in the front room;

   rain on the window on a Sunday
   afternoon;
   Dad under the bonnet of his precious
   Range Rover;
   the two dogs sitting at your feet as you
   eat your tea watching *Cartoon Time* on
   a Saturday evening;

   late night suppers with my brothers,
   when we cleared mum out of all the
   bread, cheese and peanut butter;
   musical instruments echoing from one
   or more rooms, trying their hardest to
   sound 'good';

   walking on an evening down the street
   to the local newsagents to buy an extra

pint of milk;
nipping to the chippy;
going out with a few friends.

I miss it, Lord.
I miss it all and more.
But I have to move on.

I'm twenty one, yet I feel eleven.
I'm that same child in an older, bigger
    body.
I still want to run in the woods,
    sit in front of the fire eating my tea,
    get toys for Christmas
    and believe in Santa Claus.

But I can't;
    or so people tell me.
'You're grown up now!'
    they say.
'Act your age!'

But Lord,
    I don't want my age to dictate my
    behaviour or how old people say I
    should act.
    I want it to be me;
    how old I am inside.

You said that if we couldn't be like little
    children we wouldn't get in to heaven.

33

And that Lord, is I believe, one of the most
    important things you said.

We should not forget our childhood days,
    leave them behind,
    act 'grown up' —
    they are a part of us.
We are all children at heart.

We all still need to be as a child:
    to hold a parent's hand,
    run through leaves in Autumn,
    wander through imaginary worlds in
    our minds
    and dream . . .

So, Lord,
    sitting here,
    I remember my childhood home.
    I dream of sitting by that fire on a
    Saturday afternoon
    watching T.V.,
    the dogs beside me
    and a glass of lemonade in my hand.

I miss my home, Lord,

    and I'm glad.

Amen.

ME . . . MYSELF . . . I . . .

Lord?
It's me again.
I'm sitting at my computer,
   in the middle of an essay,
   and I've got a problem.
It could wait.
After all, this essay is for tomorrow.
But I need to talk about this now.
It's bothering me and I need to chat about
   it.

It's me, Lord,
   me;
   my self obsession,
   my self-centredness,
   my infatuation with what is happening
   to me
   whilst I forget about others:
   my friends,
   people,
   other people with problems too;

   problems that don't matter when
   compared to mine;
   problems that are quite frankly
   irrelevant when put next to the enormity
   of my own;
   problems which I don't have time to

deal with at the moment because I have
'other things to do';
problems that *they* should be able to
deal with,

not dump them on me;

problems that they should put aside for
mine,

offer me a helping hand,
give me the pity *they* deserve,
the warmth *they* need to feel,
the hand *they* want to hold,

the shoulder *I* have not offered,
the ear *I* have not opened,
the heart with which *I* haven't even cared.

Because, Lord,
    all that is really important
    is me,
    myself,
    I;

    my own self-importance,
    my own need to be adored,
    admired,
    loved.

I want them to come to me,

to ask *me* how *I* feel,
to know when *I* need help,
when *I* am feeling under the weather,
tired,
worn down.

But in this, Lord,
I fail to recognize what they have offered.
In their need I see
    selfishness.
In their loneliness I see
    begging.

So, Lord, I come to you,
    the friend who always listens,
    always helps,
    always waits
    unquestioning,
    full of love.

And I ask you, Lord,
    that in my selfishness,
    my ignorance of others,
    my self obsession,
    you will offer me, not the helping hand
    that I myself find so hard to stretch out,
    but help me to notice the others who are
    hurting,
    needing me,
    myself . . . I.

Amen.

37

THE CHILD IN THE ADULT

Lord,
I'm standing here,
   arms hanging by my sides,
   legs tired and weary.
My hair dangles,
   bedraggled and
   dusty.
The shoes on my feet are worn,
   seams coming apart,
   soles flapping.

The cuffs of my shirt lie opened,
   exhausted,
   the button on the left
   missing.

And I stand here,
   at the end of a journey . . .
   . . . the beginning of another;

   the journey till now of
   education;
   the one to follow of
   careers,
   lifestyles,
   houses,
   televisions.

And I look back and see the path I took
   alongside the one I should have
   followed.

As a child the paths coincide,
   carefree innocence guiding me along the
   way,
   inquisitive,
   mischievous,
   exploring.

I followed without knowing,
   merely trusting,
   looking no further
   than the next adventure,
   the next discovery,

   be it pond or tree,
   bike ride or den,
   not out of choice,
   not from being told,
   but because that was the way to go,

   to reach out and touch the world,
   drink in its beauty,
   its mysteries;
   to swim in the rivers of enjoyment,
   to laugh and giggle,
   running through the fields of happiness.

Then later I see where one path begins to
    stray slightly;
    not far,
    but enough.
When I began to question
    the reasons for going,
    the path to follow,

I discovered I had made a choice,
    that I needed reasons
    beyond blind trust;
I needed answers
    beyond discovery.

So I questioned a little,
    rebelled a little,
    strayed a little.

And got lost a little.

But still I held on to the path I had
    followed for so long.
I could always remember where I'd left it,
    where I'd been before.

But as I grew,
    and my mind looked out from behind
    my eyes,
    so I took bigger strides,
    with longer legs,

saw new things I wanted to explore
with the childhood innocence
I once had,
but which had now changed into
adult curiosity.

And even though curiosity killed the cat,
    the cat had nine lives.

So I always looked for more;
    more to see,
    more to do,
    more to explore,
    taste,
    feel,
    smell.

So the paths grew further apart.

I became lost.

And it was only when lost,
    when confused, hurt and frightened,
    that the path was led back,
    guided again,
    to head in the right direction.

It was only when the choice I had
    discovered
    left me only one option,

that I fell back to that childhood way;

held out my hand
and stepped blindly back
on to the right way:

The RIGHT way.

So here I am,
    at the end of that journey,
    the beginning of the next,
    beaten and torn,
    tired, dusty,
    but standing facing the right way,
    a way which is hidden from sight;
    a way which holds untold mysteries,
    unanswered questions,
    undiscovered countries.

So I ask you,
    my Lord,
    as I put my hand in yours,

    to guide me,

    the child in the adult . . .

Amen.

DROWNING

Lord,
I'm lost.
I've come so far
    and now I've lost my direction.
I thought coming to college was a good idea:
    further my education,
    increase my chances for employment,
    have a laugh for a few years.
But I can't help wondering if I've made the
    wrong choice.

I guess you're tired of hearing this one:
    students tired of their lot,
    confused,
    lost,
    undecided as to the meaning of their life.

Well, I'm another of them,
    one of the many, no doubt;
    sick of the system,
    tired of the teaching,
    yearning to experience life outside the
    classroom,
    see the real world,
    leave behind pointless essays
    on irrelevant subjects,
    taught by lecturers

who have never lived in a
real world,
in an institution existing only
for its own self gratification.

I don't want this.

I'm swimming towards an island which I
    created that doesn't exist anymore;
    an island sitting in a sea of questions
    that float unanswered;
    an island that holds the dreams
    that I've forgotten;
    ideals that I've mislaid,
    futures I've wished for
    and watched float over the horizon.
    I'm swimming, Lord,
    but I'm beginning to sink.

I'm tired, Lord,
    and all I want is to stop,
    let everything wash over me
    as I sink to the bottom
    and drift without a care.

Hold my head above the water, Lord.

Don't let me drown.

Amen.

THE GIG!

Lord,
    my ears hurt,
    my knuckles are bleeding,
    and my neck refuses to allow my head
    to turn!

And I really smell . . .

To say 'Guess wot I've been doing?' would
    be to invite ridicule.
If you don't know, then you must be hard
    of hearing!

Lord,
I think that between myself and three of
    my friends we have re-invented the
    meaning of noise pollution.
We have just finished possibly the noisiest
    and smelliest sounding gig in the history
    of human kind!

There were three bands playing.
The first were pretty good musically but a
    bit dull to watch —
    no stage presence,
    no movement,
    just music . . . if you like that sort of
    thing.

The third band were one of those blues
    bands which seem to exist solely
    on doing cover songs from
    the 'Blues Brothers'.
The crowd seemed to enjoy it —
    easy to listen to
    and pretty good for a bop.
    (Boring if you ask me.)

Then there was us —
    three lads and one lass
    and a lot of enthusiasm!

The sound check was interesting.
Before the gig each band had to do a check
    to give the sound technicians a chance
    to set the sound levels, etc.
The other two bands took about an hour
    each to get their sound 'just right'.

We took five minutes.

When asked what we wanted,
    all our lead guitarist said was,
'We'd like it loud with loads of feedback
    please!'
And that is exactly what we got
    though it's hard to tell if that is what the
    crowd wanted.

Actually it isn't.
They just stood there as these four idiots
    took the stage and proceeded to run
    around, beat their instruments into a
    pulp and laugh a lot!

It was great!

Marti (the one on lead) is known to be
    rather less obvious than myself —
    quietish and unassuming.
Yet, put a guitar in his hand and a
    frightening transformation takes place.
The man is mad!
I almost felt sorry for his guitar!
It was not so much being played as being
    systematically destroyed!
After much running around and trying to
    make the most disgusting noise ever by
    hitting his amplifier with what was left
    of his guitar, he then decided to throw it
    in the air, let it land with a thud on the
    floor and proceed to hit it with a pair of
    my broken drumsticks!

Not entirely normal behaviour.

Trev (on bass) had never done a gig before.
He had been pretty nervous during it and
    spent most of his time standing still and

thumping out heavy bass riffs
(like most bass players do anyway!).
Yet once we were called on for an encore
something happened.
He suddenly decided that it would be a
good idea to run on stage, pick up the
bass and hit one string as hard and as
quickly as possible for as long as
possible or until he was drowned out by
the rest of us!

He looked even more surprised than the
audience!

And whilst this was going on, Mandi (lead
singer/screamer) was jumping in and out
of the audience and I was standing up
behind my kit hitting it as hard as my
drumsticks would let me!

It was a stupendous night! —
loads of noise,
loads of dancing,
loads of screaming and

LOADS OF FUN!

So, Lord,
although we may have kept you awake
all night,

given you and numerous others
earache
and torn apart at the seams
the meaning of the word 'music',
I can't help but feel that even if we were
      the only ones who enjoyed it,
I wouldn't have missed it for the world!
I thank you for it!

Amen.

LECTURES

I've doodled four sides of A4,
    made five paper aeroplanes,
    played hangman,
    noughts and crosses,
    even 'spot the bald patch';
    and the lecturer is still speaking.

I've looked out of the window,
    chased raindrops down the pain,
    watched other lives drift by in silent
    pictures,
    trees talking to the wind;
    and the lecturer is still . . .

I've dived into the sunshine,
    swum through the rain,
    spotted clouds change
    to friends I've never seen;
    and the lecturer is . . .

I've been trapped upon a cellophane sheet,
    displayed upon the wall,
    felt my back burn under the gaze of
    millions,
    melting my black ink scrawl;
    and the lecturer . . .

I've drifted in to multicolours,
    through stars and flashing lights,
    floated on a raft of models and theories,
    praying my answers to be right;
    and the . . .

I've crossed out all my ambitions,
    cut circles in my mind,
    watched the world walk by
    on the other side,
    laughing and leaving me behind;
    and . . .

    and, and, and,
    and . . .

    and I am still here,
    trapped inside my mind,
    in this room,
    on my own in this crowd;

    asking questions about my life,
    about the future,
    whether I'll be here tomorrow.

Will I make the grade?
What if I drop out?
Why don't I understand?
Who can I talk to?

Who will I see tonight?
Why is my pen running out?
Have I forgotten to hand an essay in?
Are my views politically correct?

Am I wrong to think 'this'?
Why is the world round?
Why am I here?
What do my friends think of me?

Am I fat?
Am I attractive?
What do I really want to do with my life?

. . . and the lecturer is still speaking . . .

Amen.

JUST ADMIRING

Lord,
I'm sitting in a lecture and I'm not
   listening.
Neither am I taking part in 'group
   discussion', 'note taking' or 'question
   answering'.
I am not sharpening my pencil, underlining
   a title or thinking that I need to ask the
   lecturer a question.

No, Lord.
My mind is elsewhere.

As are my eyes.

You see, Lord,
   sitting in a room with two hundred
   other students allows you certain
   advantages.
And I'm making full use of them, Lord.
One could almost say that I am admiring
   your artwork,
   enjoying your masterly creation,
   soaking up the heady atmosphere as I
   gorge my soul upon the sights of silent
   beauty before my eyes.

One could also say that I am
   girl watching,
   checking out the talent or
   ogling!

Call it what you will, but I'm doing exactly
   that and loving it!
Hip hip hurrah! for yet another one of
   your great ideas — attraction!
I'm sure I am not the only enthusiast —
   even in this room!
   Sitting in the silent privacy afforded by a
   lecture presents a perfect hide of
   camouflage!
Armed with only your eyes the hours can
   seem to just whizz by as new details
   flutter into sight!

And it's the little details that count.

You see, Lord, in a lecture you can be
   pretty much on your own.
Unlike being out with friends where the
   company often results in loud 'Fwars!'
   and elaborate scoring systems,
   being on your own lets you take in the
   more intricate details.
You have more time to watch,
   observe —

the way someone (that girl over there
with the straight jet black hair)
sits slightly forward,
chin resting on her hand,
chewing slightly the end of a pencil;
that wonderful way some hide
behind a curtain of hair,
doodling on the note pads;
those two in the corner, whispering.

Now, Lord, I'm not being disrespectful,
    or sexist.
I'm just doing what people have done
    throughout history,
    man and woman alike;
    from the days of Adam to the days of
    fast food,
    looking and loving from afar,
    not getting involved,
    just admiring.

And I thank you for it, Lord;
    for giving us the pleasure of each other,
    for the pleasure of just looking,
    for the joy in just innocently watching.

    . . . and especially for that girl over
    there staring at the wall!

Amen.

IN BED AT 11 A.M.

Lord,
I've skived today.
I woke up late,
    didn't hear the alarm clock,
    and missed the lecture.

Whoops.
What a shame.

Can't say that I'm all that bothered.
One and a half hours of 'the history of the
    national curriculum and its
    implementation in today's society'
    doesn't really cause me to jump up and
    listen.

I can't help it.
It's boring,
    dull,
    uninteresting,
    anti-stimulatory.
If I'd've gone, all I'd have come back with
    would be four A4 sheets of gibberish I'd
    never read, interspersed with comments
    on the sadness of the lecturer and at
    least 30 games of hangman.
An unnecessary,

uninteresting,
'important' part of my degree.

Important?
How?
Why does so much that we learn seem not
     only to be irrelevant but taught by
     people totally disconnected from real
     life?

Where do they come from?
Why are they all so dull?
And why are they so convinced that they
     are all so terribly funny?

I don't get it.
They stand there wearing brown everything
     except for the tie which has to be really
     brightly coloured so as to appear 'cool,
     hip and trendy'.
Their shoes are worn out.
Chalk dust filters through their pockets.
Some even close their eyes whilst talking to
     the students who they appear to think
     all sit on the far right in the wall ten feet
     up!
And they use theories and models and
     overhead projector films bathed in
     words like:

diametric

procrastinate
prelimination
and
ablorimanitationaryizmnessable

(And they wonder why we ask questions!?)

I'm not being disrespectful, Lord.
It's just that at times I feel that if they can't
    be bothered to make it interesting then
    why should I bother going?

So here I am,
    at home,
    still in bed,
    thinking about breakfast,
    asking, Lord,
    just one small favour.

. . . please, Lord, don't let that happen to
    me . . .

Amen.

IN A CORNER CRYING

Lord,
It's been a long time since our last chat —
    a very long time.
I'm sorry.
I've really missed our little chats;
    the support you gave,
    the friendship,
    the love.

And now I'm back,
    knocking at your door,
    asking to be let back in,
    tears in my eyes,
    dirt on my feet and hands,
    begging to be washed again,
    by you,
    my Lord,
    my friend.

I'm sorry that I wandered away,
    left home,
    went it alone;
    because,
    as always,
    I've made a mess of things again,
    and I've no choice but to come running
    back,

crying for help as, once again,
I get swept up
in my own insignificant,
selfish
problems.

I've wanted to talk for a long time now;
    day after day,
    trying to get back,
    and failing to do so;
    needing something to draw me back in.

Lord?
Why do old feelings never die?
I thought I was in control.
That was then.
This is now.
And at first it was:
    no problems,
    coping fine.

And then . . .

Lord,
I don't understand myself.
I complicate everything;
    let my feelings rule.
I wish I could turn them off,
    shut them down.

But I can't.
And every now and again,
    POW!
The bubble bursts,
I'm shot to pieces,
    blown apart by my own thoughts.

And the monster is released:
    the monster of jealousy,
    the monster of self-pity,
    the monster of silenced pain,

    the monster of myself;

    created by me:
    my thoughts,
    my actions,
    my problems,
    my own inadequacies;

    held back only by my pride,
    my stubbornness,
    my image;

so easy to escape.

And it does.

Screaming and yelling,
    it tears through me,

ripping me apart from the inside.
I try to control it,
    but . . .
    . . . it has control over me,
    takes over,
    and I'm swallowed up,
    swept up in a mass of confused,
    frightened,
    lonely

    solitude,

    as I find myself in a corner,
    faced by the monster,
    of me;

    trapped like a wounded animal.

And there is nothing more dangerous than
    an animal wounded,
    frightened,
    and trapped . . .

So I fight,
    in the only way I know how:

    verbal abuse,
    sarcasm,
    double meanings,
    innuendo.

All to protect me;
    stop anyone seeing what I'm
    really thinking;
    prevent anyone breaking through,
    seeing inside the shell,

    the shell of happy-go-luckiness,
    of cool calculated-ness,
    of helpful advice for friends who want
    to talk and need someone to talk to;
    the shell hardened
    to anything getting in and . . .
    anything getting out.

Because inside is a child sitting in a corner
    . . . crying.

Doesn't know why;
    too many reasons,
    some small and insignificant,
    others heartbreaking;
    some new,
    others old.

But all are there.

And instead of sharing them,
    asking for help,
    they are coped with

    alone.

People ask why?
Get angry when there is no response,
    when they don't understand.
      So they leave the child in the corner.

All it needed was a knowing,
    silent,
    loving,
    caring,
    embrace;
    true warmth of friendship.

Then perhaps the child would speak.
But the child is silent.
And I am silent.
So, Lord,
I come to you . . . in my corner.

Amen.

CROWDED

Lord,
    can you see me?
It's pretty crowded down here;
    people milling everywhere,
    desperate to get where they are going,
    or not as the case may be.

I feel shut in by the enormity of the crowd:
    thousands everywhere
    and me . . .
    . . . in the middle.

I'm down here,
    lost in the waves of people
    washing up on the shore of life,
    separate lives flowing along different
    channels,
    taken by changing currents,
    drifting off in to numerous horizons.

Lord,
    can you hear me?
I'm shouting above the sounds,
    the screams,
    the yells,
    the voices of lives everywhere
    needing attention,
    help.

I'm screaming to be heard
    and to hear a reply;
    to be told what I'm doing is right,
    that it isn't all a waste of time,
    that there is a purpose,
    a need for me to be alive,
    a need for me to continue along the
    road I've chosen,
    a need for me not to give in,
    put my paper and pen quietly down
    on the desk,
    get off my chair,
    walk out of the room
    and shut the door.

Lord,
    can you touch me?

Can you reach out and put your hand in
    mine?
    embrace me?
    protect me?
Can you get close enough in this crowd?
Can you push your way through the bodies
    to me?

Lord,
    in this crowd,
    this swirling mass of ever changing
    confusion,

I find it hard to understand how you,
my Lord,
can come to me.
I fail to see through my eyes, which are
rarely open,
how, in the midst of millions,
you have the time,
the power,
to come to my aid;
to drag me out of this crowd,
allow me to breathe again.

So I ask
in the silence of my mind,
hidden by the living, breathing crowd,
that on the tide of life
you will never lose sight of my hand
stretched above the heads of millions,
reaching out for you.

Amen.

!?!##¤!**?!

Now Lord, I'm not wishing to be
    outspoken,
    out of line,
    rude,
    crass,
    or out of order.

But I have a question —
    just one —

    a tiny little niggle which has crept its
    way forward in my mind,
    a minuscule problem.
Nothing much.

But I was just wondering, Lord,
    (just a little),
why it is, that if I am at college with the
    supposed cream of the country,
    the pick of the crop,
    the top two percent or whatever,
    that after all that work I put in,
    the time and the effort and struggle
    to pass exams and get here,
    why it is that now,
    more than ever before in my entire life,
I have to endure more people than I ever

thought possible,
who are (and I ask you please to forgive
me for this little outburst)

COMPLETE AND INSUFFERABLE PRATS!

I'm sorry Lord,
I guess that was rather inexcusable.
But I think you know me well enough to
    understand me even when I lose my rag
    a little.

I know that we are all created
    differently —
    individuals.
    independent in thought, word and deed.
But are we all really expected to 'get on'?
Because if we are,
    I'm not doing too well.

I can't help it, Lord.
Occasionally the patience
    just runs a little dry.
My ability to smile and be friendly
    stops a little short of the goal.
And I can't help but want to scream
    at them,
*'How did **YOU** get here?!'*

And I mean it, Lord,
    even if it is wrong.
Now I'm not saying that everyone is like
    this —
    not at all.
Just that there are too many of those who
    are.

The ones who think they are really great,
    your supposed gift to everyone:

The ones who are so damn (sorry, Lord)
    loud!
The idiots.

The 'I've been there, done that' crowd.
The show-offs.

Those who believe it is 'really cool, man' to
    eat cold pizza which is two days old,
    covered in brown sauce to give
    it some taste.

The ones who spout off about their
    political views,
    and tell you yours are wrong.

They drive me MAD!

I'm sorry, Lord.

I want to be patient;
    to listen and try to understand;
    to hold back when my temper begins to
    rise and remember that perhaps those
    who I find so nauseating might actually
    think the same

    . . . of me.

Amen.

THE BANK MACHINE SPOKE
TODAY

The bank machine spoke today.
'Overdrawn,' it said,
    minus pounds flashing upon the screen,
    money I'd spent that I didn't have.

I thought that I'd been careful,
    but I guess not.

So that's it, really:
    twenty pence per day left.
Well, almost.

Now, Lord,
I don't want to plead poverty.
I can't bear it when students do.
They usually have no idea as to the
    meaning of the word 'poor'.

But I do want to complain.

The trouble is, Lord,
    who to?

My voice is lost along the hall of
    bureaucracy,
    echoing from the walls until the

meaning is lost,
falling silently on deaf ears.

But I want to have my say, Lord;
    not just for me,
    not just for the money,
    but the principle.

Lord,
    education is everyone's 'right',
    from street kid to lord and master.
It is not something that you pay for.
To buy something limits your buying power
    to the size of your wallet;
    the bigger the wallet,
    the more you can buy.

That's fine if it's a luxury:
    a car,
    a house,
    new clothes.

Not education.

It is wrong, Lord.
Wrong.
Why should someone with more cash be
    able to get a better education than
    someone with less?
Education should provide a base to
    stand on;

73

a platform where all are equal;

given equal chances,
opportunities.

Why then Lord, should the grants be cut?
Why take from those wanting to learn?
There should be provision for everyone,
    regardless of their background.

All should have this chance.

Work hard and get there.
Use that chance to study,
    to learn.

But take away the grant?
Increase the loan system?
Why?

'Honest,' they say,
    'it's for the best,'
The best for who?

For those who are turned away by the fear
    of an overwhelming loan?
For those whose parents will not support
    them?
For those who can't afford it?

No, Lord,

I think not.
It is not for the best.
If it was,
    we would all benefit,
    gain.

But here we have a selection.
If you can pay,
    you can get it.
If you can't,
    they will not listen.

I don't want to leave college in debt.
I don't want to see money that I earn
    disappear.
When I earn I will be taxed,
    just like everyone else.
This money will then go to
    health care,
    the police,
    the fire service,

    education,

    giving someone else that chance
    to learn,
    the same chance that I had.
That should be my payback.

I work.
I earn.

I get taxed.
I provide for others.
We all provide for each other.
That is what it is about.

This society speaks about equality,
	opportunities for all,
	rights for all.
Where are our rights if we end up paying
	for our education?
	our health?

Your wallet will define how much you learn.
Your wallet will open or close the doors to
	the hospital.
Your wallet.
Your money.

And Lord,
	we will divide.
This 'classless' society will split.

The wealthy,
	fit,
	well,
	highly educated,
	paying for their children to become
	fit,
	well,
	highly educated.

And those less well off?

Well, Lord,
    they'll shout.

They'll scream,
    and yell,
    to be given the same chance,
    the same opportunity;
    to get there;
    to be equal.

Will their screams continue to bounce
    along the halls of bureaucracy,
    falling silently on to deaf ears,
    while they shout Lord?

Let them be heard.

Amen.

CHEERS!

At this pint (!), Lord, I would like to have
    said, 'My friend and I did really well;
    how clever we've been;
    we have used our minds and our
    cunning eye for opportunity.'
Yet this is not so.
We have failed somewhat.
Our business venture has flopped.
Our plan for domination of the market has
    fallen flat on its face.

We had decided that seeing as we were
    'poor students'
    it would be a 'really good idea'
    to try and brew our own
    beer.

It seemed fail-proof at first.
We already had the kit.
My mate had done it before.
Everyone was saying how easy it was to
    do; and how cheap!
So off we set, one sunny Saturday morning,
    large wooden spoon and 'Boots' Best
    Bitter' in hand,
    to find the land not of milk and honey,
    but rather cheap beer.
We succeeded.

If this beer was to be sold then it would be
    so cheap that people would probably
    pay you to take it from them!
It was foul!
    (Tasted nearly as bad as lager!)

Now I guess you're wondering why I am
    telling you this;
    why I'm bending your ear to something
    which seems trivial and unimportant.

It's just that I wanted to say thanks for
    giving me these times in my life —
    the fun we had brewing it (we stank the
    halls out for days!);
    the excitement as we counted down the
    days to the impending arrival of the
    'Master Brew';
    the tears of laughter as we sat and
    stared in amazement at the bottles
    before us —

    forty pints of completely undrinkable
    beer!

You see, Lord, it's not the big things which
    are important,
    but the small —
    those times you share with people close
    to you;

79

the fun and laughter.
the unspoken trust.

All these things stick with you, Lord.
All these things, these memories and
    experiences
    are a part of me,
    a part of what I am.

The people I meet,
    the things I experience,
    the love and the pain —
    all these things make me what I am.

A bloke in his twenties who, although
    rather strange at times and confused at
    others,
    is very happy that you saw how to make
    him grow and enjoy life.

(Yet unfortunately you didn't give him the
    oh so necessary skills to brew decent
    beer!)

Amen.

DOUBT

Lord,
    it is quiet now
    and I am alone,
    away from the noise,
    away from the people,
    away from the distraction,

    the confusion.

So I am here
    in the darkness of my mind,
    the quietness of my room,
    to talk to you;
    to listen to you;
    to try and understand.

It seems, Lord, to me,
    that all I ever do is
    doubt:
    whether it is you or myself,
    my ability or your love,
    your existence or my trust.
I always doubt.

Some say that it is normal,
    that it allows you to question,
    search for a deeper meaning.

But with me it is consuming.
It takes over and I get swallowed.

And as it takes over,
   so my mind loses sight.
As the paths turn into lost walkways
   and the distant truth flickers and dies.

So why do I doubt, Lord?
Why do I doubt?
Is it because I want everything now and get
   upset when it takes that little bit longer?
Is it because I am too easily distracted?
No, Lord.
It is deeper than that.

It is because as I sit here and stare into the
   future,
I see the shadows of my past;
   all the memories of a childhood which is
   fading,
   sinking into the sands of my life.
It is because I teeter on the edge of an
   unknown quantity —
   my life.
It is because I see no escape from all the
   pressures, all the problems which scream
   inside my head.
I see no direction,
   no plan,
   no future.

Yet I know that this is where I must go.

My life leads on into a land that as yet I
    cannot see:
    a land full of ups and downs,
    lies and truths,
    doubts and beliefs.
And it is here that I must go.

So I find that even in my doubt,
    I rely on you:

    the one I lose sight of,
    the one I ignore,
    the one I lose belief in,

    the one that I trust.

Amen.

IT'S NOT ABOUT BEING PERFECT

Lord,
I'm tired.
I'm tired of the world;
    tired of the pressures,
    the falseness,
    the lack of faith.
I'm sick of it all.

I try.
I really try to follow you,
    to live the way that you taught,
    do the right thing.
And all I do is fail,
    trip up,
    fall flat on my face.

. . . Do you know what keeps tripping me
    up, Lord?

Not you,
    not life,
    but the way other 'Christians' perceive I
    should behave,
    act,
    be 'Christian'.
And I can't.
I can't live up to their expectations.

I'm me;
full of anxieties,
problems,
lies,
hidden secrets.

But I still hold on.

I can't pretend to be anything else.
I'm not perfect.
Why should I be?
You never asked me to be.
It's something out of reach.
. . . and I'm too far away to try.

And I'm sorry, Lord.

But others don't accept that.
They condemn,
    scorn,
    judge.
And I crouch in the corner,
    protecting myself:
    what I am,
    from what they want me to be.

I can't be what they want me to be:
    totally perfect,
    clean,
    no problems;

totally,
utterly,
completely
Christian.

And I'm not.

According to them.

But why?
Because I disagree?
Because I'm not perfect?
Because I break the rules?

But I admit that.
So what's the problem?
Didn't you come for sinners?
    for the lowest of the low?

I'm fed up, Lord,
    fed up with all these hidden judgements.
'If you are a Christian you should be
    perfect.'
But Lord, I'm only young.
I've my whole life ahead of me.
If I stopped making mistakes now,
    struggling,
    arguing,
    what would I have left to learn?

If I stopped questioning,
      going my own way,
      how would I be able to experience life
      to its full?
If I stopped being what you created me to be,
      what would I have left to give?

I live.
I experience.
Life is not about being perfect,
      it's about learning,
      following,
      following . . .

Lord,
I am not perfect.
I break the rules,
      walk my own way,
      ignore you,
      shut you out.
But I admit that.

I admit that I am nothing special.
I can't live up to what is expected;
      be perfect;
      stop doing all those 'unchristian' things.
I'm human —
      a human in a world of confusion.

Yet I still hold on to your hand.

When I'm lost,
    when I'm cold,
    when I find myself alone,
    kneeling,
    crying,
I know you'll be there.

I know that you love me.
That no matter what I do,
    no matter how sad or pathetic I become,
    that you'll be there,
    and you'll pick me up.

So, Lord,
    in my world,
    a world being destroyed by ideals that I
    follow —
    even though I may be wrong,
    I know that you want me to keep going.
So, Lord, I pray,

'Don't give up on me.'

Amen.

THROWN OUT

Lord,
I've just been thrown out,
    asked to leave.
'Don't come back . . .'

Not college.
The house I live in —
    well . . .
    . . . lived in.

The landlord asked to see me.
'Nothing personal,' he said,
    but it would be preferable . . .
    . . . if I didn't come back.

It's funny really,
I've only been here for six weeks.
Most of the time I'm out.
My room's fairly tidy . . . (honest . . .)

Yet I've been asked to leave.
So now I've nowhere to call home except
    where my parents live,
    . . . three hundred miles away.

I could commute . . .
    . . . by aeroplane.

Perhaps not.
I guess I'll just have to start looking for
    somewhere else.
The thing is though, Lord,
    I'm still rather confused as to why I
    have been thrown out!

Do I smell?
    (I shower . . . well, most days!)
Do I have wild parties?
    (Yes . . . in other people's houses!)
Do I play loud music at unsociable hours?
    (No . . . my stereo is bust!)
Do I walk rudely into other people's rooms
    and rummage through their stuff?
Do I walk up the stairs too loudly?!

WHY HAVE I BEEN THROWN OUT??
I guess I can cope with it, Lord.
I find it quite funny really.
In some ways I wish I *had* had all those
    wild parties!
At least to have a couple of real reasons for
    being thrown out!

But, Lord,
    what must it be like to be thrown out if
    you've missed your rent payments?
If your house has been repossessed?
Where do you go then?
What if you don't have a family — where

do you go then?

Is there anywhere to go?

There should be
    government funded hostels,
    somewhere to go while you sort it out,
    a place where help is freely available.

But I can't help wondering, Lord,
    that it isn't there;
    that people are left out in the cold,
    thrown out,
    cast out,
    living amongst the rubbish on our
    streets.

I've been thrown out, Lord.
But I've somewhere to go;
    people who'll help me.
I'm not alone.

Help me to remember that
    and to remember those others who have
    found themselves thrown out,
    but without warning,
    those on our streets,
    alone.

Sit by them, Lord.

Amen.

THE HOUSE I'M GOING BACK TO ...

Lord,
I'm sitting in my car,
   on my way home for a break —
   the Christmas holidays.
I've packed my bags,
   filled the car to the brim,
   and left the house.

But there is one small problem.

The house I've left isn't the one I'll be
   coming back to.

I have nowhere to go
   when term starts again.
I'm on my own,
   no house to go to,
   and I'm scared.

How do I look for a house?
Where do I go?
Who do I ask?

I've tried already;
   went to the college,
   asked them for help.
You'd think that they'd be able to give a
   hand.

But the list of vacancies was empty,
    all the houses gone.

No houses left except one or two.
One required females only;
    the other a house for four.
So I'm on my own,
    stuck.

Homeless?
Surely not.
But I am.
After all, I can't live at home and go to
    college.
I have to live here.
But where?

Where?

I can't afford anything else.
I tried the estate agent.
They asked if I was a student.
Suddenly, I wouldn't be able to pay weekly,
    or monthly,
      but six months up front.

I wish that they had just politely shown me
    the door,
    asked me to leave,
    instead of making me feel insignificant,

unworthy,
unwanted.

I need a place to live, Lord,
   so I can go to college,
   continue my course,
   get a degree,
   a job.

But what if there isn't anywhere?
What do I do?
Jack it all in?
Go home?

Is this happening to me?
I can't believe it.
All these people
   driving their cars
   to their houses
   in their little worlds,
   and me
   driving home
   with nowhere to come back to . . .
I know, Lord, that I'm not as badly off as
   some.
I know that there are others with no home
   at all
   except the street,
   the doorway,
   under the bridge.

But I'm not comparing myself to them.

Maybe through all this I'll be able to
    understand a little more —
    empathise,
    know a little more about what they are
    going through.

But Lord,
    amongst all their pain,
    their loneliness,

    please remember me . . .

Amen.

DISAPPEARING UNDIES . . .

Lord,
I did my washing today!
HURRAH!
But somehow,
    (and I really don't understand this),
    my underpants are missing.
And so are three socks.

Do you know where they are?
You see, Lord, it's one of those bizarre
    occurrences.
You know you put them there.
You are sure that they were spotted
    entering the washing machine,
    being shoved in to the dryer,
    yet,
    against all the laws of nature,
    you open up the bag when you get home
    and lo and behold

    . . . they are gone!

They that were there are no longer in your
    possession.
They have taken it upon themselves to
    explore further avenues of work,
    explore the world,

go out and meet other single pieces of
underwear!

Weird.

Where on earth did they go?
Is this another one of those hilariously
    amusing heavenly humours?
Another angelic jape?
Something to tickle the ribs of all wearers
    of halos?

(Imagine losing *those* in the wash!)

I know you have a sense of humour,
    a definite interest in the sublime and
    divinely daft.
One only need look at other classics of
    God-funniness —

    acne,
    men having nipples,
    my face.

You are one comical creator!

So where do they go, Lord?
Why do they disappear?
Are they all in heaven?
And that's why I'm praying, Lord;

Not because I want my underpants back,
(although it would be helpful),

but just to say thanks for giving us all
something to laugh at —
from people to places,
jokes to japes,
laughs to tears of happiness,

and back to my disappearing undies!

If at the end of my life I can look back
with you, Lord,
sitting down around an old camp fire,
crack open a bottle of wine,

and,
amongst all the mistakes,
the mess,
the problems,
the pain,
see the fun as well,
I will know that I have lived . . .

Amen!

TADPOLES, MULTIPLICATION AND DIVISION!

Lord,
I'm sitting on a bus,
    at seven o'clock in the morning,
    on a Monday,
    and it's raining.

I'm a student teacher —
    a breed of people who for one reason
    or another made a decision,
    a simple one,
    one that would affect all their time at
    college.

Instead of going for a normal degree
    which involves eight hours of lectures
    a week,
    we decided that a degree which
    involved full days of lectures and
    week after week of teaching practice
    would be much more fun.

We would leave college with a degree
    and a qualification too.
We would learn organisational and
    communication skills,
    develop techniques which would

allow children to discover their true
capabilities,
be involved in a job which is challenging
and enjoyable.

No one mentioned *this* though, Lord

The programme goes as follows:
you get up at between six and half past
to catch the bus.
Two hours later you arrive at your school,
unless you are really unlucky and your
school is only half an hour away
which means waiting for the doors to be
opened or sitting in a cold classroom for
an hour and a half listening to the boiler
coughing its way into life.

A day at school ensues, which consists of:
getting very high on caffeine,
being enthusiastic about everything from
tadpoles to multiplication and division;
trying to develop an air of authority
whilst at the same time letting the
children know that you are friendly and
willing to help;
knowing how to spell every word in the
English language,
teaching every subject perfectly,
justifying everything according to the

aims of the National Curriculum;
keeping an eye on Karl, Damien,
Jenny and Kylie,
keeping count of all the pencils, rubbers,
rulers, books, stencils,
multi-links and sets of compasses;
and at all times setting a good example
by dressing neatly, not losing your
temper or swearing.

Then it's another two hour journey back to
college to arrive home at just after six.
Tea follows.
Then we have an evaluation of each lesson,
marking all the school work,
tomorrow's lesson plans and . . .
'The Making of the Packed Lunch'.
Then, finally, bed!

Doesn't that sound like fun?

To be really honest, Lord, there are times
when I feel like giving up,
jacking it all in.
But I don't.
And it's when I think of the reasons why I
don't that I see perhaps a little bit of
(dare I say?) 'fun' in what I'm doing.

When the children say they are really

enjoying the lesson;
when a child who has been really
struggling with something finally
understands;
the look on their face as they realise that
they've got a really great mark;
when, after the first few days of chaos,
the class accept you as their teacher and
actually
listen!
perhaps even a chat at playtime with
one of the quieter ones —

It is at times like that, Lord, when the early
mornings and very dull sandwiches seem
unimportant.
You begin to feel that perhaps you are
doing better than you thought,
that you can actually teach!
(and that the children like you!)
There are also the times with all your
friends going through the same —
the horror stories;
helping each other with ideas;
swapping lesson plans;
chatting on the bus on the way home;
relaxing in front of the T.V. and
forgetting for a little while the days
ahead;

the atmosphere;
the moments of success;
the friendships that help the long days
seem a little less severe;
encouragement from your teacher and
tutor.

All these things, Lord, make it not seem so
bad,
that perhaps amongst all the hard work
and annoying children
there is reward;
that I am, after all, doing something
worthwhile.

So, Lord,
on this cold morning,
sitting on a bus whose heating system
doesn't work,
I ask you to remember all student
teachers everywhere,
in the hope that you will,
in your mercy,

. . . stop Karl from walking around the
classroom when I'm talking!

Amen.

MY COLLEGE YEARS

Lord,
I know that I've complained a lot to you
    lately,
    whinged on about things,
    moaned.

But I want to say thank you
    for my college years.

You see,
    even though all I seem to do is grumble,
    these years are probably some of the
    most precious that I will ever have.

When I think of the things that I've done
    and the people I've met,
    I feel happy:
    the fun and the laughs,
    the adventures and experiences,
    even the lectures and the lecturers!

Now, Lord,
I don't want this to sound all false and
    insincere,
    one of those awful 'Thank you for this
    and that and nah! nah! nah!' prayers.
I don't want it to sound conceited either:

'Look at me and what I've done!'
isn't what I'm trying to get across.

I just want you to know that I am grateful
for the opportunities I have had
opened for me;
for all the things I have done,
and learnt about,
and experienced;

for having had the chance to live with
and get to know friends that I will
treasure for the rest of my life . . .
even though we may lose touch;

for the memories which fill my mind
with moments I will cherish for ever;
for all these things, Lord.

For all these things . . . leave me lost for
words.
And, as I sit here looking at my college
years,

I thank you Lord.

Amen.

TO BOLDLY GO . . . .

Lord,
  this is Student David J. Gatward of the
  bedroom 'Slobberprise'.
My voyage . . .
  to explore strange new fungus inside
  coffee mugs,
  to meet new levels of dribbling,
  gigglesome inebriation,
  and to boldly go . . .

Er. . . Lord?
You got a minute?

This 'boldly going' business.
Do I have to?
You see it's rather comfortable down here
  at the moment.
I have everything I need or could ever
  want,
  (except that racing green convertible
  TVR Chimaera that I mentioned last
  night),

So why does the world demand that I get
  up and go somewhere?

I don't really want to.

It's nice here:
    pub just up the road,
    great friends,
    laughs,
    late mornings,
    good food, (except when you know
    who's cooked it . . .),

    relaxation.
    no real pressures,
    no unnecessary excitement.

Complete
    and utter
    blissful,
    contentment,

    which I will soon have to leave behind
    when college ends and I find myself
    opening the door to
    the world outside . . .
    . . . my bedroom door.

And it all looks rather frightening.

It's big out there . . . . . .

I feel unprepared for what lies ahead.
I always thought that I'd feel different as
    an adult.

But I don't.
I am still that child of five entering school
for the first time.

Except this school is a lot bigger,
and a lot more frightening.

Lord,
have you ever been on a fairground
ride?
or done bungee jumping?

Well,
life at present is just like that moment
before the harness clamps you into the
seat
and you're actually on that ride.

Before you looms what appears to be two
hundred miles of very angry metal . . . .

. . waiting . . . .

. . . drooling . . . .

. . . . thirsty . . . .

Then suddenly —
WHOOOOOOOSH!!
You're off!

But I'm not at the 'whoosh' bit yet, Lord.

And it all looks very frightening.
There are dangers out there,
    things that can take over my life —

    a career,
    a mortgage,
    a marriage,
    children?
    and a garden plot!

Lord!
    Is there no escape?
These are adult things,
    adult experiences!

I'm still too young!
Look at me!
I could be all of the above before I'm
    thirty!
I could be happily married with children,
    a house, a lovely garden
    and a next door neighbour
    called Gerald!

But is life really like that Lord?
If I am here to live and to learn,
    I want to.

I want to experience what lies beyond my
    bedroom door,
    like the fairground ride.
It all looks so big,
    so terrifying.
    but once you're on
    and the excitement takes hold,
    you wonder why the thought
    of not having a go
    ever crossed your mind.

The thrills that are out there.
All the fun of the fair!
And it's free!
God given!

I *am* frightened Lord.
I really am.
But out there lies even more of the fun I've
    been having for the previous twenty two
    years!

And if that's anything to go by then I want
    some more —

    new people to meet,
    new experiences to be a part of,
    whole unwritten chapters of my life just
    waiting to be filled in!

So Lord,
    as I step on to the fair ground ride
    of life,
    and stare ahead along the tracks of
    the future,
    I ask of you just one small favour . . .

make sure I don't fall out . . .

Amen.